T0016438

**DINOSAUR
Academy**

# Adding and
# Subtracting

ARCTURUS

# Key skills in this book

ARCTURUS

This edition published in 2022 by Arcturus Publishing Limited
26/27 Bickels Yard, 151–153 Bermondsey Street,
London SE1 3HA

Author: Lisa Regan
Cover illustrator: Beatrice Costamagna
Interior illustrator: Claire Stamper
Editor: Donna Gregory
Designer: Linda Storey
Managing Editor: Joe Harris

ISBN: 978-1-3988-1987-0
CH010344NT
Supplier 29, Date 0422, PI 00001003

Printed in China

# Introduction

Welcome to the Dinosaur Academy! Join the dinosaurs and their prehistoric friends as they set out to discover just how mega-fun mathematics can be!

In this book, you'll find lots of fun activities that will help you with adding and subtracting numbers. Start at the beginning, where you will learn the basics with numbers up to ten, and then work through the book. As you go, you'll gain more and more confidence to help you get better at addition and subtraction—even with big numbers! So grab your pencil, put your thinking cap on, and let's set off on a mathematics adventure!

# Count on us!

Help the dinosaurs with their 1—2—3s
by writing the numbers here.

| 1 | 1 | one | one |
|---|---|-----|-----|
| 2 | ___ | two | ___ |
| 3 | ___ | three | ___ |
| 4 | ___ | four | ___ |
| 5 | ___ | five | ___ |
| 6 | ___ | six | ___ |
| 7 | ___ | seven | ___ |
| 8 | ___ | eight | ___ |
| 9 | ___ | nine | ___ |
| 10 | ___ | ten | ___ |

# Dino detective

Complete each of the three dot to dots
to reveal what the dinosaurs are looking at.

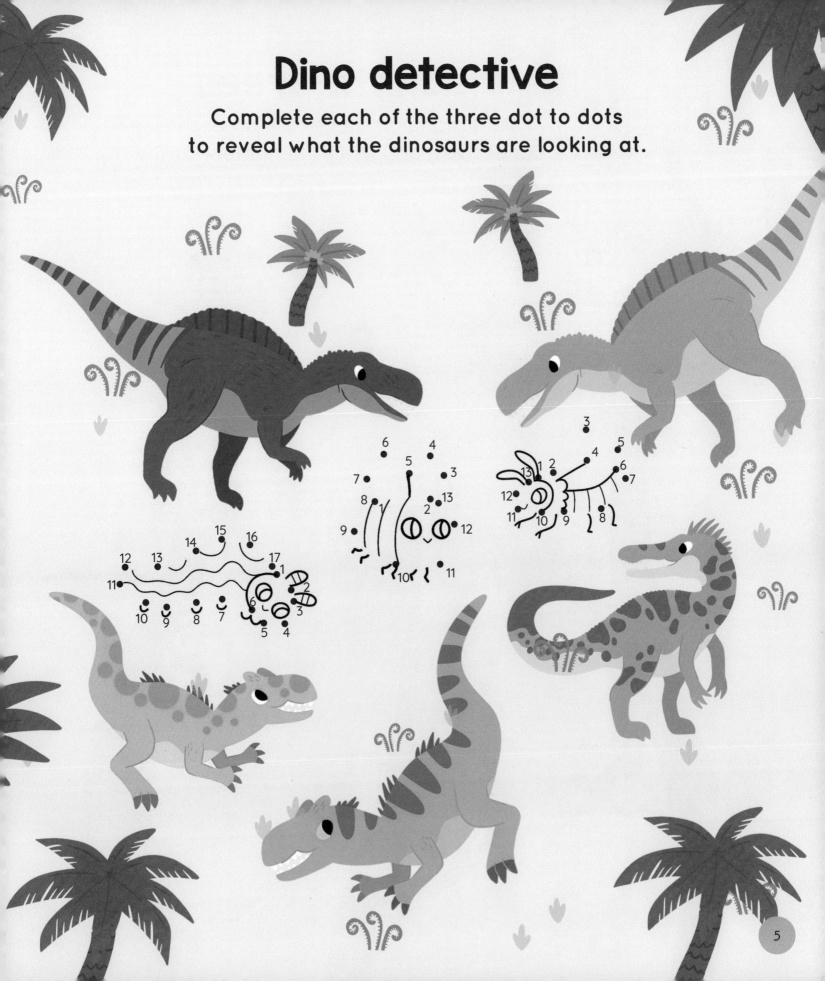

# In the trees

How many creatures are on each tree?
Count them and write the number at the top.

# Watery world

Help the swimmers count the sea creatures,
and write the numbers in each box.

# Ready, Steggy, go!

Fill in the missing numbers under each Stegosaurus.

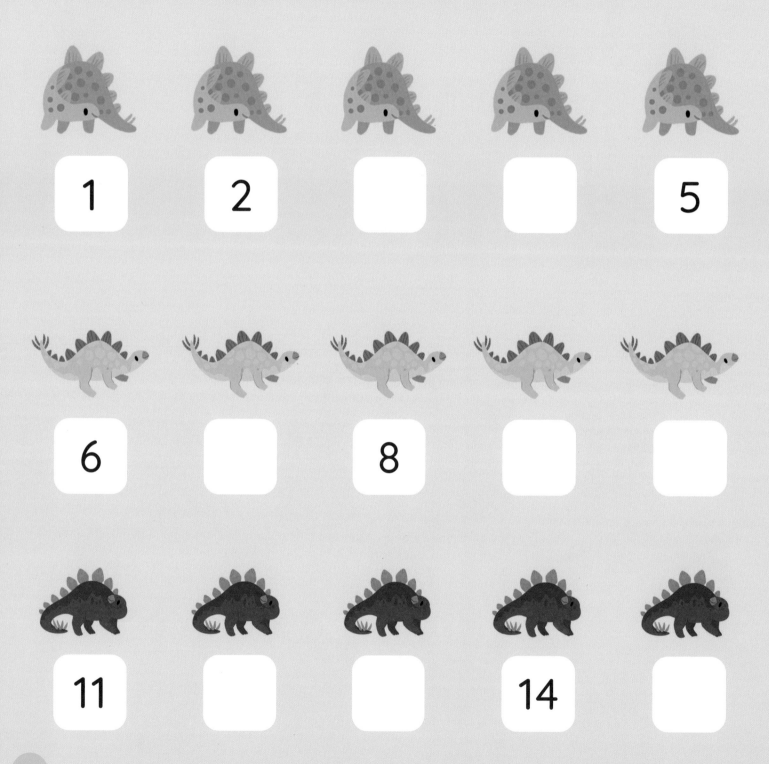

1 2     5

6   8    

11     14  

# Fill the gaps

Write the missing numbers in the circles on these smiling sauropods.

1  2  ⃝  ⃝  5  ⃝  ⃝  8

⃝  2  ⃝  4  ⃝  ⃝  ⃝  ⃝  9  ⃝

⃝  ⃝  ⃝  5  6  ⃝  ⃝  ⃝  10  ⃝

# One more

Add one more each time, writing the numbers in the boxes.

Row 1: 2, 3, 4, ☐

Row 2: 4, ☐, ☐, ☐

Row 3: 7, ☐, ☐, ☐

Row 4: 9, ☐, ☐, ☐

# Add and subtract

Ace your addition and subtraction by writing numbers that are one less and one more each time.

| one less (subtract 1) | | one more (add 1) |
|---|---|---|
| | 2 | |
| | 6 | |
| | 3 | |
| | 5 | |
| | 8 | |
| | 9 | |
| | 4 | |
| | 7 | |
| | 10 | |

# Dotty dinosaurs

Count from 1 to 27 to finish the picture of this fun, dotty dino.

# Fancy flyers

Count the flying reptiles in each group
and add one more each time.

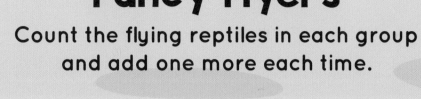

| 2 | + | 1 | = | 3 | | | + | | = | |

| | + | | = | | | | + | | = | |

| | + | | = | | | | + | | = | |

13

# Hoppit!

Take away one frog from each group.
How many are left?

5 - 1 = ☐

3 - 1 = ☐

7 - 1 = ☐

3 - 1 = ☐

6 - 1 = ☐

# Spiky subtractions

Cross out one spike from each of the Kentrosaurus.
Then work out how many spikes are left.

9 - 1 = ☐      ☐ - 1 = ☐

☐ - 1 = ☐      ☐ - 1 = ☐

☐ - 1 = ☐      ☐ - 1 = ☐

# In a line

Use the number line to solve these problems with Lucy Lambeosaurus.

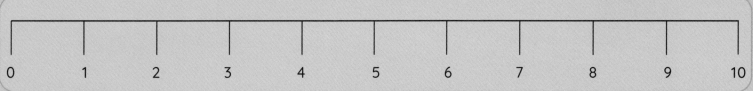

2 + 5 = ☐                5 + 2 = ☐

7 + 3 = ☐                6 + 1 = ☐

4 + 2 = ☐                1 + 9 = ☐

7 + 1 = ☐                6 + 3 = ☐

3 + 2 = ☐                4 + 3 = ☐

# Number nests

Hop from nest to nest to help Coco
and Chico solve the addition problems.

1  2

1  2  3  4  5  6  7  8  9  10

If a little pink lizard scuttles across two
nests, what number does she get to?

$1 + 2 =$ 

1  2

1  2  3  4  5  6  7  8  9  10

If a baby blue lizard scuttles from nest
4 across two more nests, where is he?

$4 + 2 =$ 

1  2  3  4

1  2  3  4  5  6  7  8  9  10

If a tiny pink lizard starts on nest 3
and jumps across four nests, where
does she reach?

$3 + 4 =$

# Getting along swimmingly

Help the Plesiosaurus with these problems
using the number line as a guide.

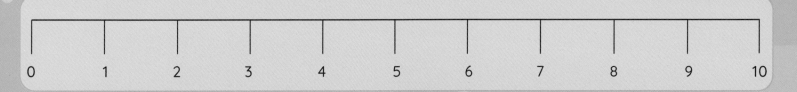

8 − 2 = ☐

4 − 2 = ☐

6 − 3 = ☐

5 − 2 = ☐

9 − 4 = ☐

6 − 5 = ☐

7 − 1 = ☐

8 − 4 = ☐

10 − 5 = ☐

9 − 6 = ☐

# Good for you

Use the exotic fruits to help Mimi count
backward and work out the answers.

3   2   1

1   2   3   4   5   6   7   8   9   10

Mimi has ten pieces of fruit. She eats three.
How many does she have now?

$$10 - 3 = \boxed{\phantom{0}}$$

3   2   1

1   2   3   4   5   6   7   8   9   10

She lets her friend Mungo have three as well. How many are left?

$$7 - 3 = \boxed{\phantom{0}}$$

2   1

1   2   3   4   5   6   7   8   9   10

Now Max eats two pieces. How many are left?

$$4 - 2 = \boxed{\phantom{0}}$$

# Number bonds

A number bond is a pair of numbers that add up to ten.
Can you write five different ones here?

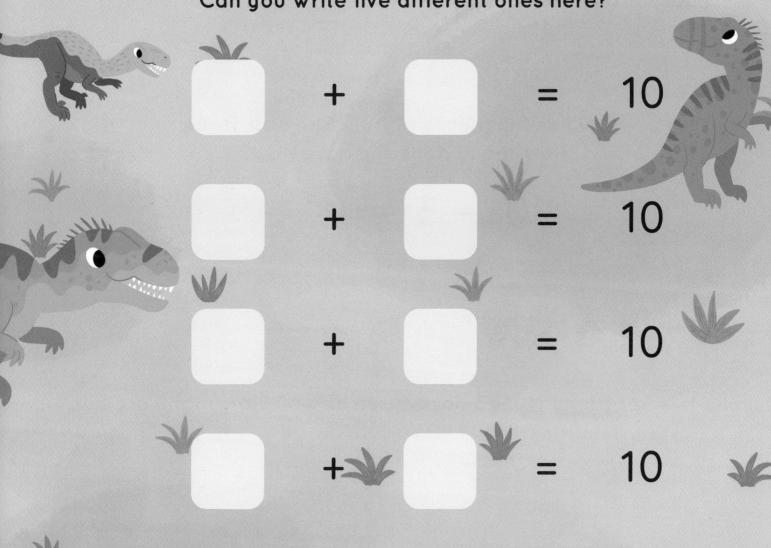

$$\square + \square = 10$$

$$\square + \square = 10$$

$$\square + \square = 10$$

$$\square + \square = 10$$

$$\square + \square = 10$$

Hey! With addition, you can put the numbers in any order. 4 + 3 adds up to the same as 3 + 4.

# Bugs and beetles

Here's a tasty snack for these Microraptors.
Draw more bugs in every group so there are ten
each time. How many have you added?

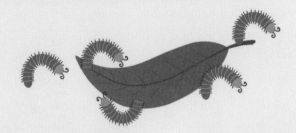

8 + [ ] = 10       5 + [ ] = 10

2 + [ ] = 10       7 + [ ] = 10

9 + [ ] = 10       3 + [ ] = 10

# Feeding time

Suni the Suchomimus needs some food!
She finds a shoal of ten fish. How many are left if ...

she eats 1?

she eats 2?

she eats 3?

she eats 4?

she eats 5?

she eats 6?

she eats 7?

she eats 8?

she eats 9?

# Bonding time

Can you remember the number bonds that add to ten?
Write them below to complete the subtractions.

10    −   ☐    =   ☐

10    −   ☐    =   ☐

10    −   ☐    =   ☐

10    −   ☐    =   ☐

10    −   ☐    =   ☐

# Special delivery

How exciting! Dippy Diplodocus and her friends have got mail.
Count the letters and parcels and add them together each time.

+ = ☐

+ = ☐

+ = ☐

+ = ☐

# Sea life

Count how many sea creatures are in each group.
Fill in the numbers and solve the problems.

☐ + ☐ = ☐

☐ + ☐ = ☐

☐ + ☐ = ☐

☐ + ☐ = ☐

☐ + ☐ = ☐

# F-ant-astic

Anton and Annie are watching the ants march past. More and more keep on coming! Can you solve the addition problems?

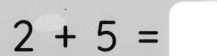

2 + 5 = ⬜

4 + 4 = ⬜

6 + 3 = ⬜

1 + 8 = ⬜

7 + 2 = ⬜

9 + 4 = ⬜

5 + 6 = ⬜

5 + 2 = ⬜

7 + 7 = ⬜

3 + 6 = ⬜

8 + 1 = ⬜

2 + 7 = ⬜

4 + 9 = ⬜

6 + 5 = ⬜

# Zero, nothing, nought

What happens when you add or subtract zero? Nothing!
Check it out with these Ornithocheirus.

Orlando loves fish. He has seven for his supper.
He doesn't catch any more. How many does he have?

$$7 + 0 = \boxed{\phantom{00}}$$

Olga loves boots! She has four boots and no one
takes any from her. How many does she have?

$$4 - 0 = \boxed{\phantom{00}}$$

Omar collects hats. He has six but doesn't
get any more. How many does he have?

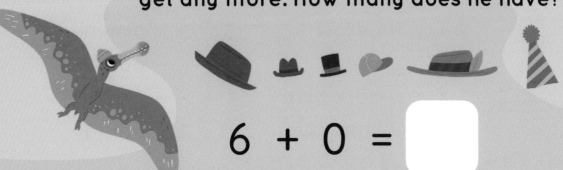

$$6 + 0 = \boxed{\phantom{00}}$$

# Paint a prehistoric picture

Solve the problems in the key and complete
the picture using the answers.

## Answer key

| | |
|---|---|
| 2 + 2 = yellow | 5 − 4 = green |
| 7 − 2 = red | 8 − 6 = purple |
| 6 + 1 = dark blue | 3 + 5 = pink |
| 4 + 2 = light blue | 10 − 7 = orange |

# A helping hand

Fill in the ammonites with the answers to help the Hadrosaurus with their homework.

2 +  = 10

 + 4 = 9

3 + 3 =

6 +  = 9

 + 7 = 8

2 + 6 =

7 +  = 10

 + 7 = 11

6 + 1 =

3 +  = 5

5 + 3 =

# Feeling hungry

Diego the Deinonychus keeps munching his snacks!
Work out how many are left each time.

(7 geckos) − (2 geckos) = [ ]

(8 sandwiches) − (4 sandwiches) = [ ]

(6 apples) − (1 apple) = [ ]

(4 bones) − (4 bones) = [ ]

# Party time

Roxy is partial to a party treat! But she knows she should share, so she gives some to her friends. How many are left each time?

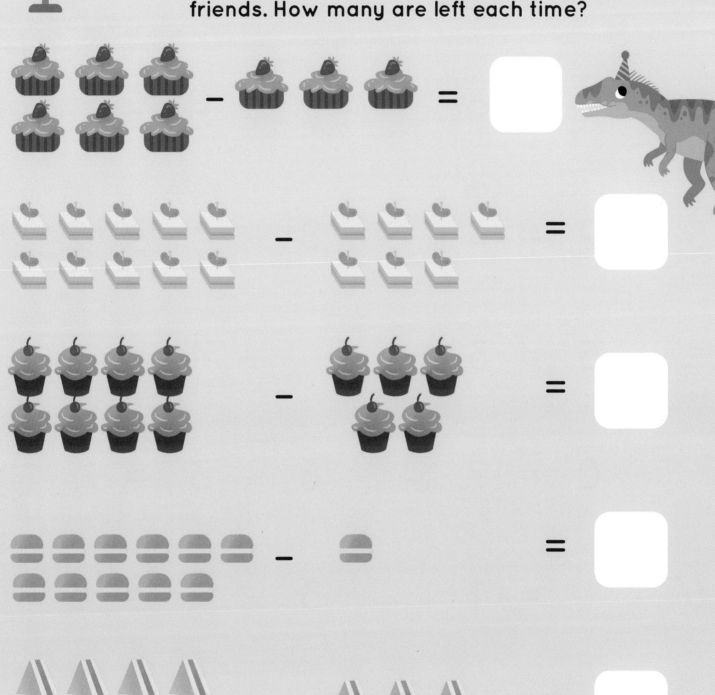

# Homework help

Trixie and Dixie need your help!
Put the missing numbers in the spaces.

9 − ☐ = 9

7 − 5 = ☐

5 − 2 = ☐

8 − ☐ = 2

☐ − 5 = 3

☐ − 4 = 6

☐ − 0 = 7

6 − 3 = ☐

6 − ☐ = 1

3 − ☐ = 3

10 − 3 = ☐

☐ − 3 = 6

# Fill me in

What goes where? Use the key to help you finish the picture.

## Answer key

4 + 2 = yellow

2 + 3 = green

7 - 4 = red

10 - 6 = blue

8 - 1 = purple

3 + 5 = orange

5 + 4 = pink

# Super spikes

Each of these Kentrosaurus should have twelve spikes in total. Does each one need more spikes or less?

15 - ☐ = 12

9 ☐ ☐ = 12

7 ☐ ☐ = 12

8 ☐ ☐ = 12

# All at sea

Should Rocco add +, -, x, or ÷ to make these problems correct?

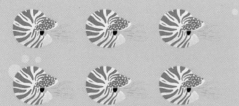  = 14

  = 1

  = 3

  = 9

  = 10

# Double trouble

Count the spots on each orange crab.
Now draw spots on each pink crab
to match. How many dots are in each pair?

4 + 4 =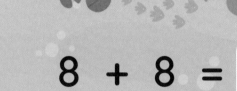

8 + 8 =

3 + 3 =

5 + 5 =

6 + 6 =

2 + 2 =

# Flying friends

If half of each group flies away, how many are left in each group? If it helps, cross out half of each group.

4 - 2 = ☐

8 - 4 = ☐

2 - ☐ = ☐

10 - ☐ = ☐

6 - ☐ = ☐

12 - ☐ = ☐


37

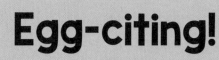

# Egg-citing!

The Maiasaura mothers are laying eggs!
If the second one lays the same number of eggs
as the first one, what is the total for each line?

$3 + 3 = 6$

$7 + \phantom{0} = \phantom{0}$

$5 + \phantom{0} = \phantom{0}$

$2 + \phantom{0} = \phantom{0}$

$6 + \phantom{0} = \phantom{0}$

# Clowning around

Coco is learning to juggle! If he drops half of the balls each time, how many will he still be juggling?

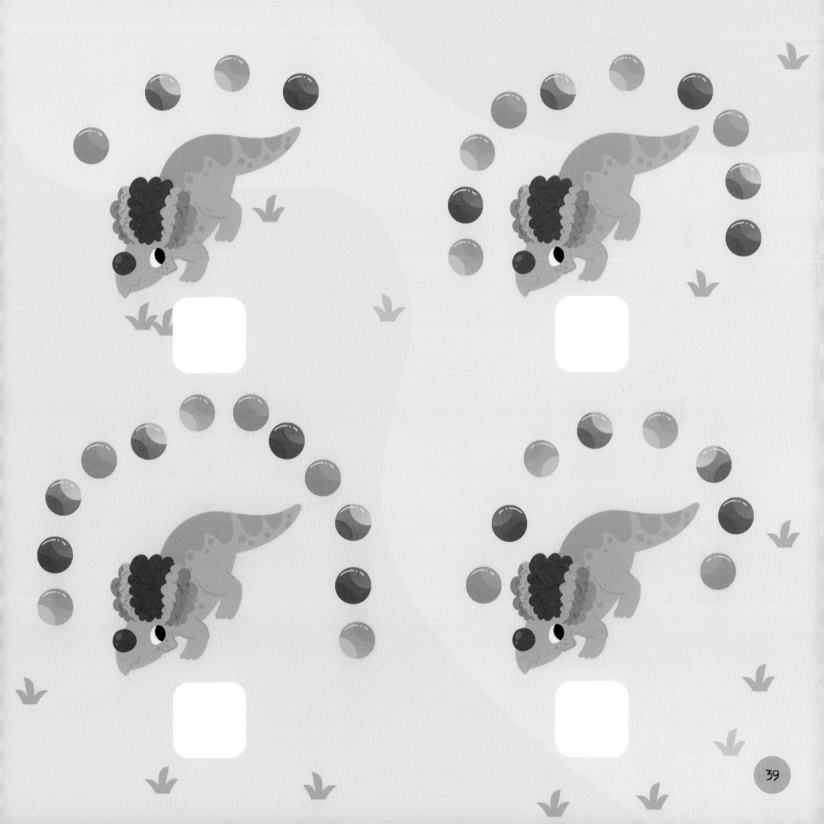

# Two by two

Only some of these problems have 2 as the answer. Which ones are they?

12 − 10 = ⬜

2 + 2 = ⬜

8 − 5 = ⬜

2 + 0 = ⬜

7 − 3 = ⬜

9 − 6 = ⬜

5 − 2 = ⬜

11 − 8 = ⬜

2 − 0 = ⬜

6 − 6 = ⬜

2 − 1 = ⬜

7 − 6 = ⬜

# Big night out

Match each of the dinosaurs to its chosen snack. Work out the answer and draw a line to the correctly numbered snack.

$8 - 3$

11

$5 - 2$

3

$8 + 3$

5

6

7

$9 - 3$

$10 - 3$

# Equal to the task

How many dinosaurs need to join the right-hand group to make it the same size as the left-hand group? Write the number in the box.

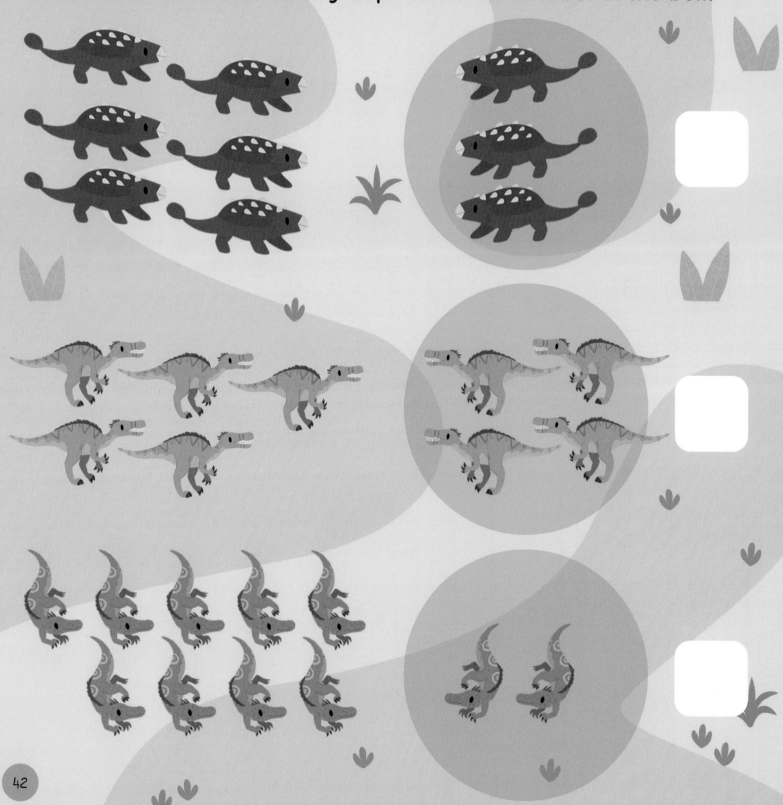

# Grubbing around

Sort the bugs and grubs so each Archaeopteryx has the same amount of each kind, and write the number in the box.

How many of each kind of creature will each Archaeopteryx get?

# Head count

Count the horns on each dinosaur and compare the numbers.
How many fewer are on the right of each pair?

# Fishing frenzy

Look at the scene below. Are there more of fish A or fish B? Fish C or fish D? Work out the difference between each pair of numbers.

A [ ] — B [ ] = [ ]

C [ ] — D [ ] = [ ]

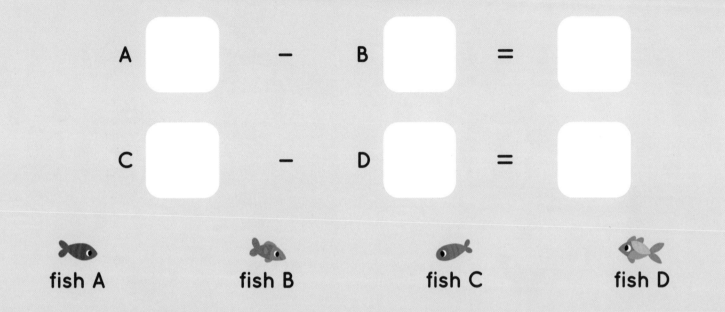

fish A          fish B          fish C          fish D

# All change

Look at the two pictures and answer the questions using subtraction and addition.

How many chrysalis are hanging in picture 1?

How many chrysalis are hanging in picture 2?

What is the difference between the two numbers?

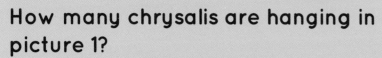

How many blue butterflies are there in picture 1?

What is the total number of blue butterflies in both pictures?

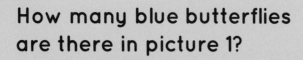

How many blue butterflies are there in picture 2?

# More or less?

Is Column A more than B, or less? Circle the answer and write in the difference, too.

| A | B | Difference | |
|---|---|---|---|
| 8 | 4 | | (more) / less |
| 11 | 12 | | more / less |
| 8 | 5 | | more / less |
| 6 | 4 | | more / less |
| 13 | 6 | | more / less |
| 3 | 8 | | more / less |
| 4 | 2 | | more / less |
| 8 | 14 | | more / less |

# On the move

Dina walks ten paces between plants to munch on the leaves. How far does she walk altogether? Fill in the distances as you count.

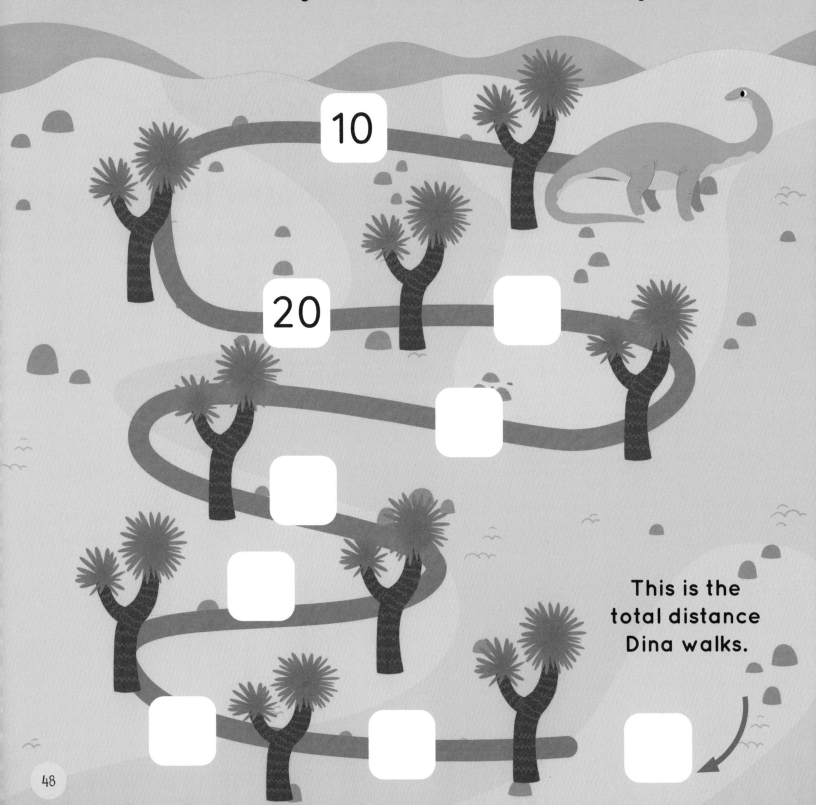

10

20

This is the total distance Dina walks.

# In a flap

Thierry can reach 20 in just two flaps of his majestic wings. Start from 0 and answer the questions as he flies.

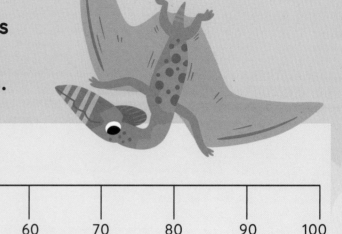

1    2

0    10    20    30    40    50    60    70    80    90    100

What number does he get to in three flaps?

What number does he get to in four flaps?

What number does he get to in five flaps?

What number does he get to in six flaps?

What number does he get to in seven flaps?

What number does he get to in eight flaps?

What number does he get to in nine flaps?

What number does he get to in ten flaps?

# All the tens

Count in tens to complete the number sequence for each dinosaur. Write the numbers in the footprints.

60

70

40

10

140

60

100

# Art school

Welcome to Arty Archaeopteryx's art school! He has carefully lined up all of his pencils in rows that are ten pencils wide, ready for class to begin. Write how many are in each group.

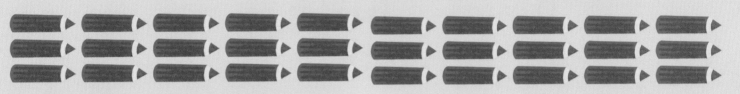

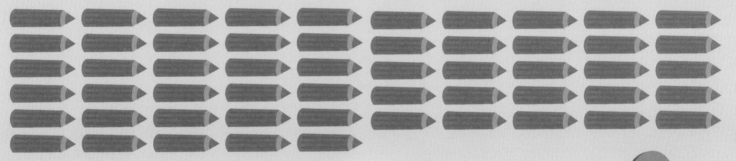

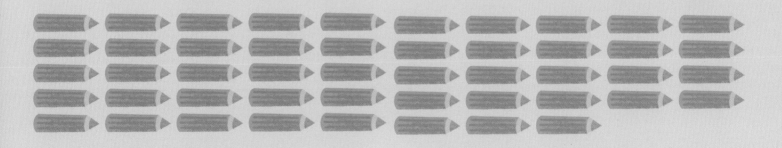

# Gone fishing

These fishing friends catch different amounts of fish—but Terence always scoops up 10. How many fish are in each catch?

6 + 10 =

2 + 10 =

8 + 10 =

9 + 10 =

5 + 10 =

4 + 10 =

# Fetch!

Join Alonso's fun by adding ten each time he collects a bone. Use the number line to help you.

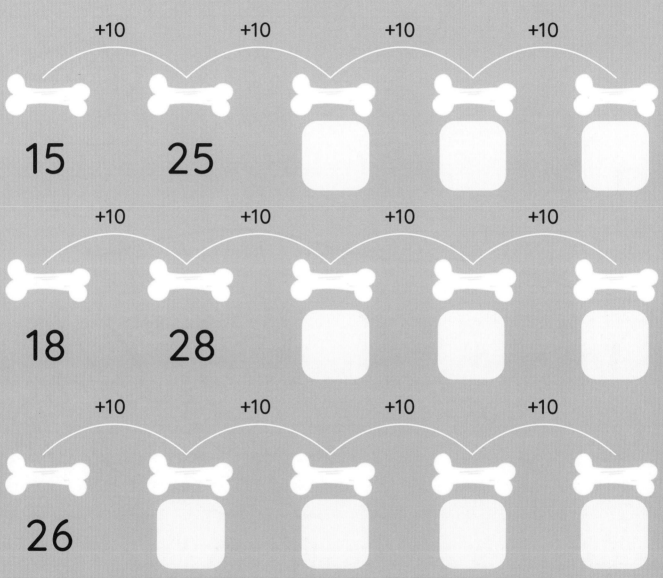

+10   +10   +10   +10

15   25

+10   +10   +10   +10

18   28

+10   +10   +10   +10

26

0   10   20   30   40   50   60   70   80   90   100

# Strange creatures

Do you know what an Ornithomimus looked like?
Join the dots, counting from 1 to 36, to find out.

# Fossil finds

Help Annie Ankylosaurus find her way to
her family by counting in twos.

2  4  6

# Bigger bonds

Number bonds don't have to make ten—they can be pairs of numbers that add up to twenty. Can you think of numbers to fill the gaps?

18 + ☐ = 20

☐ + 3 = 20

6 + ☐ = 20

☐ + 15 = 20

16 + ☐ = 20

Remember! When adding, the numbers can go in any order.

# Perfect partners

Find pairs of dinosaurs with numbers that add up
to twenty. Draw lines to match them together.
Can you spot one with a baby?

# Back to class

Arty is teaching night school this time!
He has arranged his pencils in groups of twenty now.
As each student arrives, they take a few pencils to
their own desk. How many are left each time?

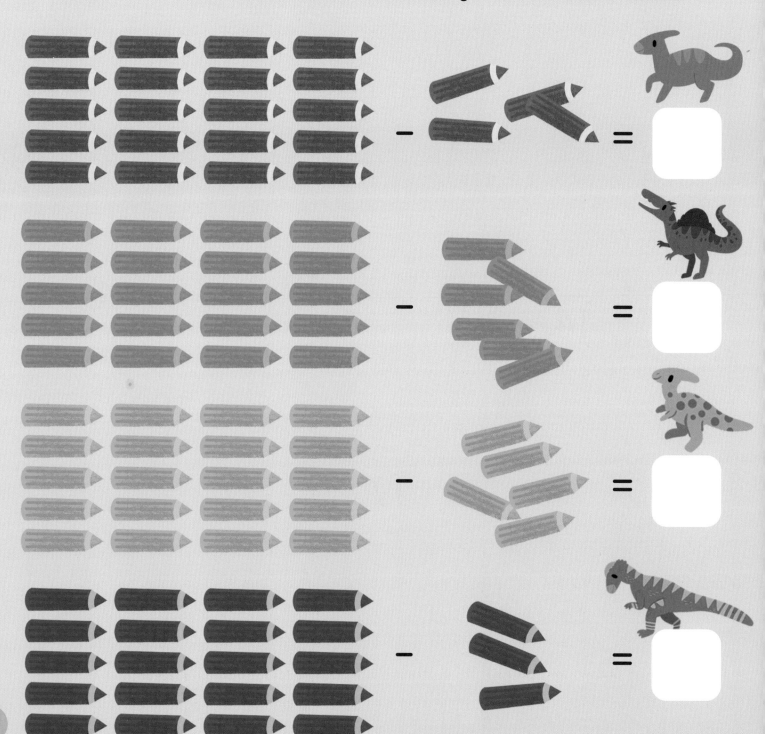

# Feeling fruitful

Help Gigi and Didi work out the missing numbers that make twenty. Write the missing numbers in the boxes.

$16 + \boxed{\phantom{0}} = 20$

$20 - \boxed{\phantom{0}} = 12$

$\boxed{\phantom{0}} + 8 = 20$

$20 - 4 = \boxed{\phantom{0}}$

$5 + \boxed{\phantom{0}} = 20$

$20 - \boxed{\phantom{0}} = 3$

$\boxed{\phantom{0}} + 11 = 20$

$20 - 13 = \boxed{\phantom{0}}$

$1 + \boxed{\phantom{0}} = 20$

$20 - \boxed{\phantom{0}} = 18$

# Add them up

Each dinosaur is worth a different amount. Simply add up what each pair is worth using the values below.

| 8 | 5 | 12 | 15 | 7 | 2 |
|---|---|----|----|---|---|

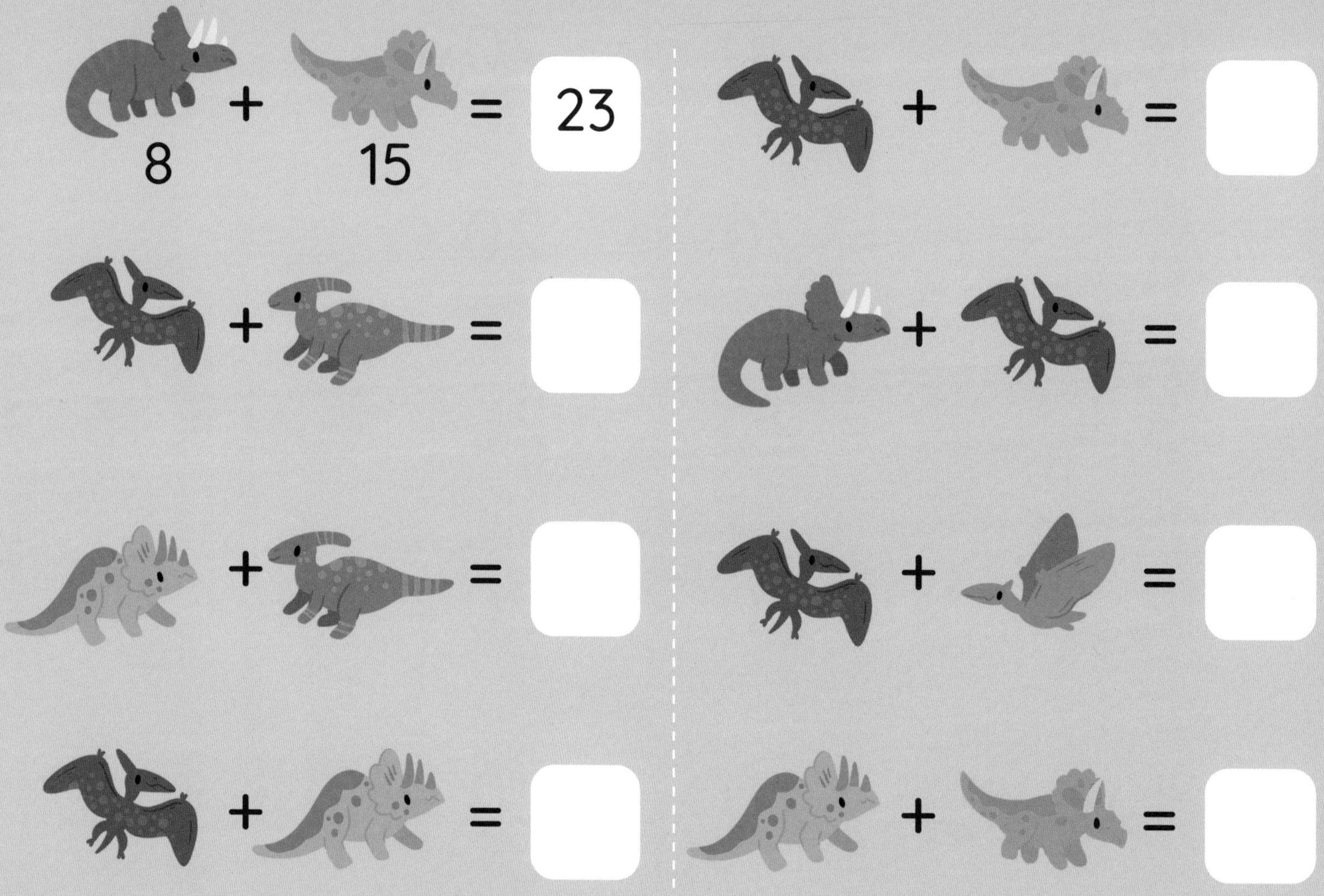

8 + 15 = 23

+ =

+ =

+ =

+ =

+ =

+ =

# Super speedy

Help Bojo and Beppo add these pairs of numbers as quickly as you can.

11 + 6 = 

13 + 1 = 

14 + 5 = 

16 + 4 = 

12 + 3 = 

10 + 9 = 

11 + 4 = 

12 + 5 = 

22 + 1 = 

17 + 2 = 

25 + 0 = 

11 + 8 = 

# Bridging through 10

Discover the answers to these problems. Use part of the second number to round the first number to 10, and then add the remaining units. Follow the example.

6 + 7 = **13**

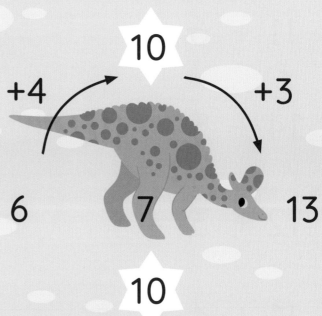

+4          +3

6          7          13

8 + 5 = ☐

+2          +3

8          5

9 + 6 = ☐

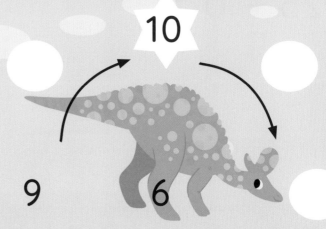

9          6

# Bridging back

Discover the answers to these problems. Use part of the second number to round back to 10, then take away the remaining units. Follow the example.

16 − 7 = 9

10

−6   −1

16        7        9

13 − 6 =

10

−3   −3

13        6

15 − 8 =

10

15        8

# Happy families

Add each dinosaur's group of numbers and then match the total to find a parent and a youngster with the same answers. Write the matching pairs in the boxes below.

A

$4 + 2 + 5 + 8 = \boxed{\phantom{0}}$

B

$7 + 4 + 9 + 2 = \boxed{\phantom{0}}$

C

$4 + 2 + 5 + 8 = \boxed{\phantom{0}}$

D

$5 + 7 + 9 + 1 = \boxed{\phantom{0}}$

 $\boxed{\phantom{0}}$ and $\boxed{\phantom{0}}$

$\boxed{\phantom{0}}$ and $\boxed{\phantom{0}}$

# T. rex teaser

Each T. rex has a cup of tea with its own answer on it. Draw lines to match them up.

11

6 + 6 =

7 + 9 =

15

11 + 3 =

16

9 + 2 =

12

14

8 + 7 =

# Safety in numbers

A huge herd of Protoceratops is on the move—
a hundred of them! If ten rush past every minute, calculate
how many are left as they head to the horizon.

How many are left after two minutes? $100 - 20 =$ ☐

How many are left after five minutes? $100 - 50 =$ ☐

How many are left after seven minutes? $100 - 70 =$ ☐

How many are left after nine minutes? $100 - 90 =$ ☐

How many are left after ten minutes? $100 - 100 =$ ☐

# Plodding along

Bruno the Brachiosaurus saunters along slowly. He covers 20 paces in one hour. How far does he go in two hours? Place each answer in the circle on each number line.

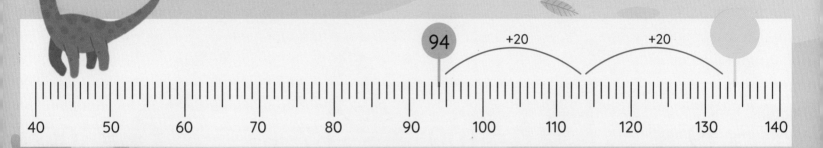

94  +20  +20

40  50  60  70  80  90  100  110  120  130  140

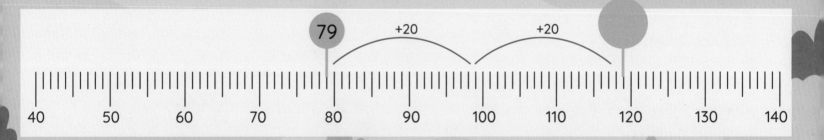

79  +20  +20

40  50  60  70  80  90  100  110  120  130  140

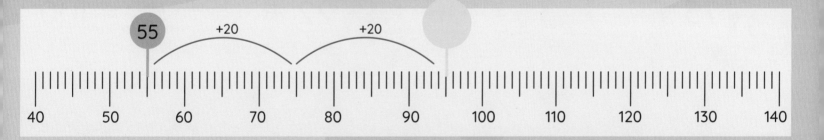

55  +20  +20

40  50  60  70  80  90  100  110  120  130  140

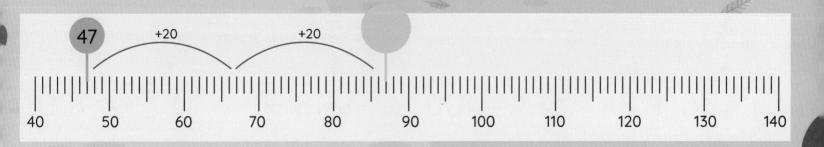

47  +20  +20

40  50  60  70  80  90  100  110  120  130  140

# Star students

Meet Theo the Therizinosaurus and Valentina the Velociraptor—both are star students! Valentina has to write a number that makes 100 when added to Theo's. Can you fill in the blanks?

19 + ⬜ = 100

67 + ⬜ = 100

75 + ⬜ = 100

22 + ⬜ = 100

36 + ⬜ = 100

48 + ⬜ = 100

# Winging it

Can you help these Rhamphorhynchus find the answers to their problems? Draw lines to the butterfly containing the correct answer for each dinosaur.

100 − 16 =

100 − 85 =

100 − 63 =

15

73

84

37

46

9

100 − 54 =

100 − 27 =

100 − 91 =

# Doubling up

Which of the numbers on Daddy Stegosaurus
is worth double the amount on the baby Stegosaurus?

20

40
44
22

33

66 99 133

400

80 880 800

# Half and half

The giant water monster eats half of each type of fish. Work out how many of each type it eats. Write the number in each box.

10

30

80

# Three by three

Each Triceratops has three numbers. Use them to fill in all of the addition and subtraction facts, like the first one.

**23**  **52**  **29**

| 23 | + | 29 | = | 52 |
| --- | --- | --- | --- | --- |
| 29 | + | 23 | = | 52 |
| 52 | − | 23 | = | 29 |
| 52 | − | 29 | = | 23 |

**25**  **41**  **16**

| | | | | |
| --- | --- | --- | --- | --- |
| | | | | |
| | | | | |
| | | | | |

**28**  **13**  **15**

| | | | | |
| --- | --- | --- | --- | --- |
| | | | | |
| | | | | |
| | | | | |

**63**  **44**  **19**

| | | | | |
| --- | --- | --- | --- | --- |
| | | | | |
| | | | | |
| | | | | |

# Triceratops tricks

The tricky tricksters have made an error on each of these answers. Can you work out what it is each time?

| 21 | + | 18 | = | 39 |
| 18 | + | 21 | = | 21 |
| 39 | − | 18 | = | 21 |
| 39 | − | 21 | = | 14 |

| 24 | + | 32 | = | 56 |
| 32 | + | 24 | = | 56 |
| 54 | − | 24 | = | 32 |
| 56 | − | 32 | = | 24 |

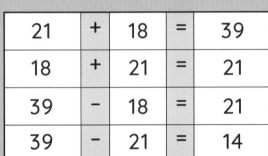

| 11 | + | 25 | = | 36 |
| 25 | + | 11 | = | 36 |
| 36 | − | 11 | = | 22 |
| 36 | − | 25 | = | 11 |

| 28 | + | 49 | = | 77 |
| 47 | + | 28 | = | 77 |
| 77 | − | 49 | = | 28 |
| 77 | − | 28 | = | 49 |

# Higher and lower

Fill in the outer columns with numbers that are ten more and ten less than the central numbers.

| ten more (add 10) | | ten less (subtract 10) |
|---|---|---|
| | 15 | |
| | 42 | |
| | 77 | |
| | 21 | |
| | 39 | |
| | 56 | |
| | 65 | |
| | 90 | |
| | 112 | |

# Top of the class

Remember Valentina and Theo, our star students?
They're back! This time, Valentina has set a challenge
for Theo. He must find one answer
that doesn't equal 16.
Can you spot it?

Double 8

6 + 10

90 − 74

12 + 4

50 − 34

Half of 32

11 + 15

88 − 72

69 − 53

# Tread carefully

Help the giant sauropod find a way to its nest by drawing a path from palm to palm. Count upward in tens.

# Fishy fun

Subtract ten to find a match for every pterosaur that has caught a fish. Draw lines to pair them up.

56

104

87

77

24

72

34

94

66

62

# Face value

Each of these Torosaurus has a different value. Which set of three adds up to the greatest amount?

13

16

20

□ + □ + □ = □

□ + □ + □ = □

□ + □ + □ = □

□ + □ + □ = □

# Prehistoric puzzler

Find a set of three dinosaurs whose numbers add up to 100. The other three dinosaurs will also add up to 100. Draw a line to connect the three dinosaurs in each set.

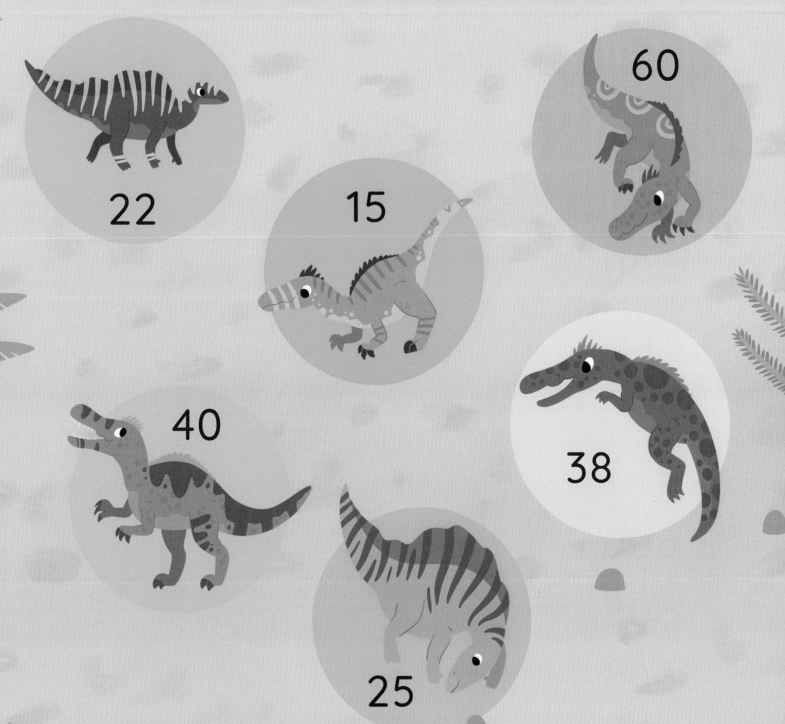

# Carnotaurus columns

Fill in the columns using
the correct numbers.

| | Hundreds | Tens | Units |
|---|---|---|---|
| 3 | | | |
| 33 | | | |
| 300 | | | |
| 13 | | | |
| 15 | | | |
| 155 | | | |
| 500 | | | |
| 505 | | | |
| 555 | | | |

# Write it right

Work out the calculation needed for each question and write it in the space.

A female Maiasaura has 12 eggs. Three of them are stolen. How many are left?

In a group of 30 Lambeosaurus, 16 are left-handed. How many are right-handed?

Euoplocephalus visits 18 eating sites in a week. How many does it visit in two weeks?

Each member of the Protoceratops herd has two special pebbles. There are 10 in the herd. How many pebbles do they have in total?

# Use your brain

What is each dinosaur worth? The totals are given for three dinos in each row or column added together.

# Dinosaur friends

Each set of three dinosaurs adds up to 200. What number is missing from each set? Use the number line to help if you need to.

60 + 70 + ⬚ = 200

120 + 30 + ⬚ = 200

40 + 90 + ⬚ = 200

20 + 50 + ⬚ = 200

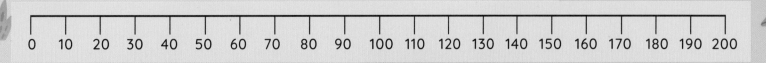

0  10  20  30  40  50  60  70  80  90  100  110  120  130  140  150  160  170  180  190  200

# How much?

Use the values of each little dinosaur to work out the answers to the picture problems.

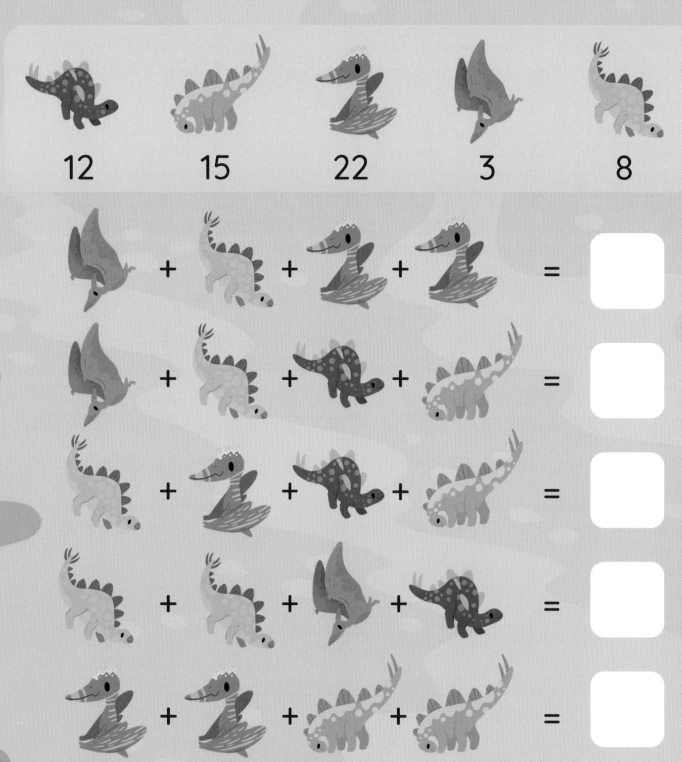

12        15        22        3        8

# Take it away

Work out the answers and write the number problems underneath each time.

50    20    13    16    27

# End of the line

Follow the instructions along the trail to
work out the final figure at the end.

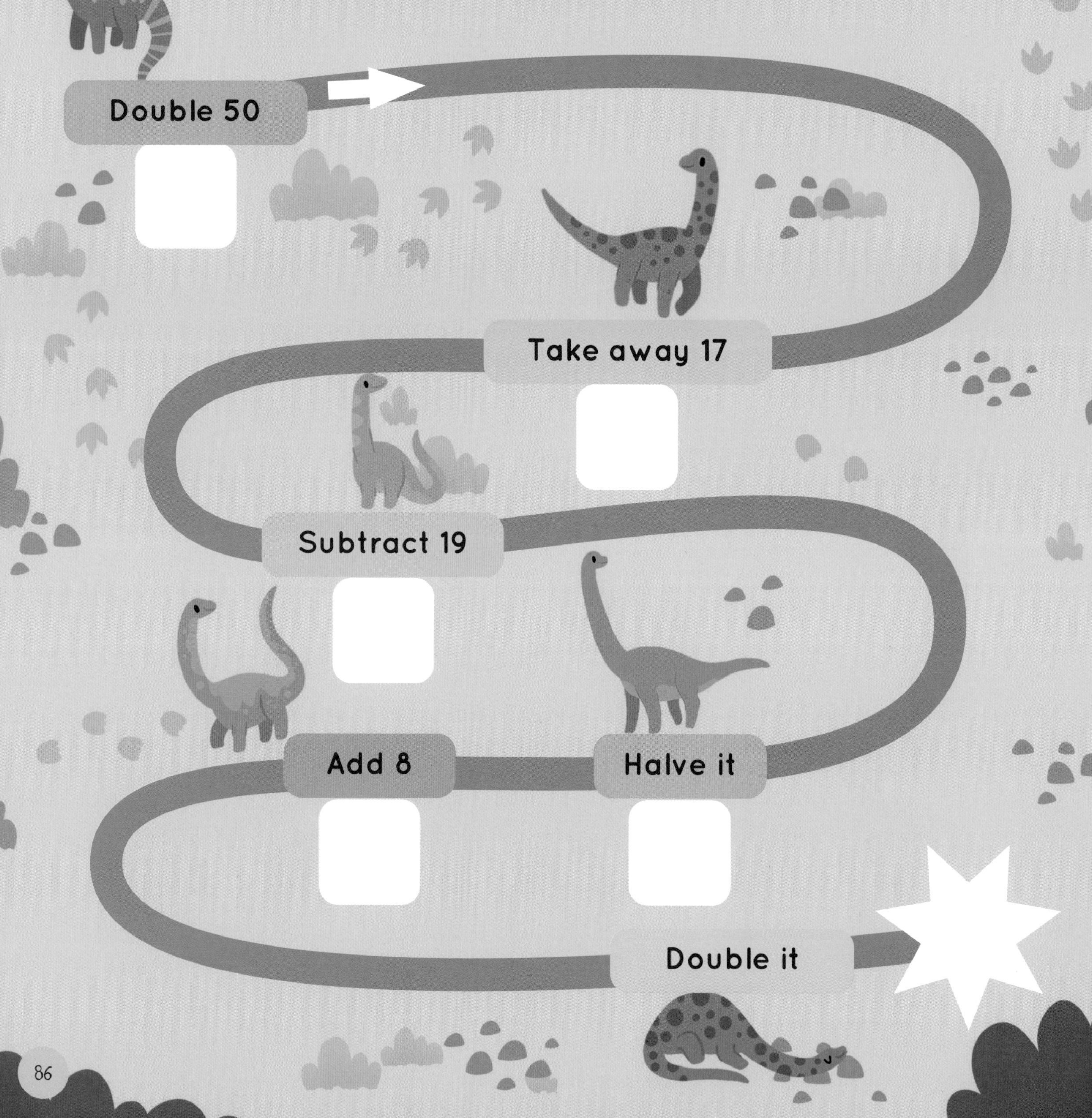

Double 50

Take away 17

Subtract 19

Add 8

Halve it

Double it

# Answers

## 5 Dino detective

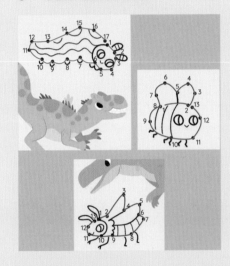

## 6 In the trees

## 7 Watery world

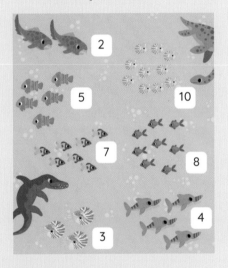

## 8 Ready, Steggy, go!

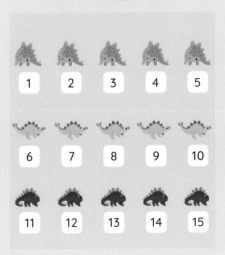

## 9 Fill the gaps

## 10 One more

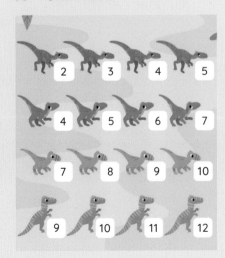

## 11 Add and subtract

| one less (subtract 1) | | one more (add 1) |
|---|---|---|
| 1 | 2 | 3 |
| 5 | 6 | 7 |
| 2 | 3 | 4 |
| 4 | 5 | 6 |
| 7 | 8 | 9 |
| 8 | 9 | 10 |
| 3 | 4 | 5 |
| 6 | 7 | 8 |
| 9 | 10 | 11 |

## 12 Dotty dinosaurs

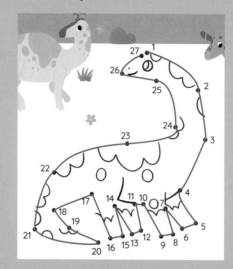

## 13 Fancy flyers

2 + 1 = 3    6 + 1 = 7

4 + 1 = 5    5 + 1 = 6

3 + 1 = 4    7 + 1 = 8

## 14 Hoppit!

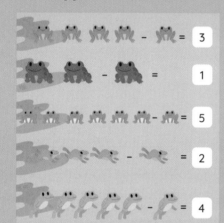

- = 3

- = 1

- = 5

- = 2

- = 4

## 15 Spiky subtractions

9 - 1 = 8    11 - 1 = 10

10 - 1 = 9    13 - 1 = 12

14 - 1 = 13    16 - 1 = 15

## 16 In a line

2 + 5 = 7    5 + 2 = 7

7 + 3 = 10    6 + 1 = 7

4 + 2 = 6    1 + 9 = 10

7 + 1 = 8    6 + 3 = 9

3 + 2 = 5    4 + 3 = 7

## 17 Number nests

1 + 2 = 3

4 + 2 = 6

3 + 4 = 7

## 18 Getting along swimmingly

8 - 2 = 6    4 - 2 = 2

6 - 3 = 3    5 - 2 = 3

9 - 4 = 5    6 - 5 = 1

7 - 1 = 6    8 - 4 = 4

10 - 5 = 5    9 - 6 = 3

## 19 Good for you

10 - 3 = 7

7 - 3 = 4

4 - 2 = 2

## 20 Number bonds

$$10 + 0 = 10$$
$$0 + 10 = 10$$
$$1 + 9 = 10$$
$$2 + 8 = 10$$
$$3 + 7 = 10$$
$$4 + 6 = 10$$
$$5 + 5 = 10$$
$$6 + 4 = 10$$
$$7 + 3 = 10$$
$$8 + 2 = 10$$
$$9 + 1 = 10$$

## 21 Bugs and beetles

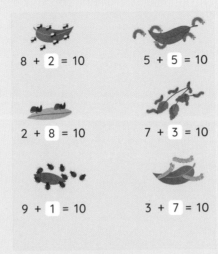

$$8 + 2 = 10 \qquad 5 + 5 = 10$$
$$2 + 8 = 10 \qquad 7 + 3 = 10$$
$$9 + 1 = 10 \qquad 3 + 7 = 10$$

## 22 Feeding time

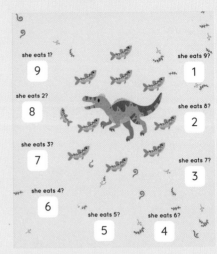

she eats 1? **9**   she eats 9? **1**
she eats 2? **8**   she eats 8? **2**
she eats 3? **7**   she eats 7? **3**
she eats 4? **6**
she eats 5? **5**   she eats 6? **4**

## 23 Bonding time

$$10 - 0 = 10$$
$$10 - 1 = 9$$
$$10 - 2 = 8$$
$$10 - 3 = 7$$
$$10 - 4 = 6$$
$$10 - 5 = 5$$
$$10 - 6 = 4$$
$$10 - 7 = 3$$
$$10 - 8 = 2$$
$$10 - 9 = 1$$
$$10 - 10 = 0$$

## 24 Special delivery

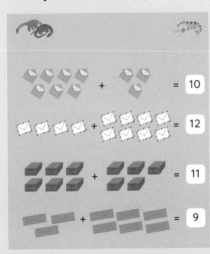

$$= 10$$
$$= 12$$
$$= 11$$
$$= 9$$

## 25 Sea life

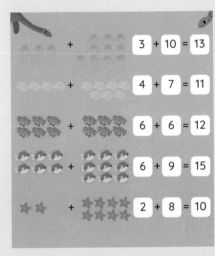

$$3 + 10 = 13$$
$$4 + 7 = 11$$
$$6 + 6 = 12$$
$$6 + 9 = 15$$
$$2 + 8 = 10$$

## 26 F-ant-astic

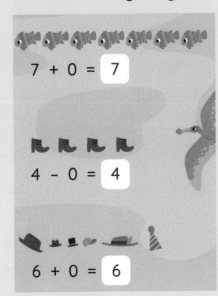

$$2 + 5 = 7 \qquad 5 + 2 = 7$$
$$4 + 4 = 8 \qquad 7 + 7 = 14$$
$$6 + 3 = 9 \qquad 3 + 6 = 9$$
$$1 + 8 = 9 \qquad 8 + 1 = 9$$
$$7 + 2 = 9 \qquad 2 + 7 = 9$$
$$9 + 4 = 13 \qquad 4 + 9 = 13$$
$$5 + 6 = 11 \qquad 6 + 5 = 11$$

## 27 Zero, nothing, nought

$$7 + 0 = 7$$
$$4 - 0 = 4$$
$$6 + 0 = 6$$

## 28 Paint a prehistoric picture

## 29 A helping hand

2 + 8 = 10        2 + 6 = 8

5 + 4 = 9        7 + 3 = 10

3 + 3 = 6        4 + 7 = 11

6 + 3 = 9        6 + 1 = 7

1 + 7 = 8        3 + 2 = 5

                5 + 3 = 8

## 30 Feeling hungry

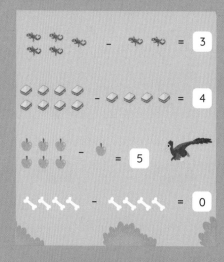

## 31 Party time

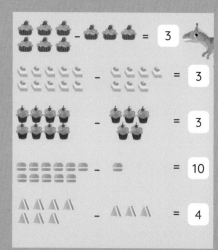

## 32 Homework help

9 - 0 = 9        7 - 5 = 2

5 - 2 = 3        8 - 6 = 2

8 - 5 = 3        10 - 4 = 6

7 - 0 = 7        6 - 3 = 3

6 - 5 = 1        3 - 0 = 3

10 - 3 = 7       9 - 3 = 6

## 33 Fill me in

## 34 Super spikes

15 - 3 = 12        9 + 3 = 12

7 + 5 = 12         8 + 4 = 12

## 35 All at sea

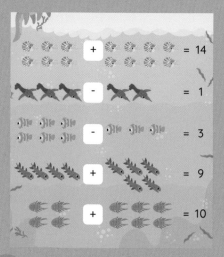

## 36 Double trouble

4 + 4 = 8         8 + 8 = 16

3 + 3 = 6         5 + 5 = 10

6 + 6 = 12        2 + 2 = 4

## 37 Flying friends

4 - 2 = 2         8 - 4 = 4

2 - 1 = 1         10 - 5 = 5

6 - 3 = 3         12 - 6 = 6

## 38 Egg-citing!

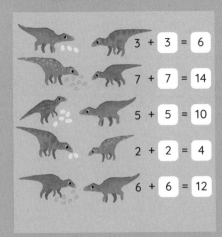

3 + 3 = 6
7 + 7 = 14
5 + 5 = 10
2 + 2 = 4
6 + 6 = 12

## 39 Clowning around

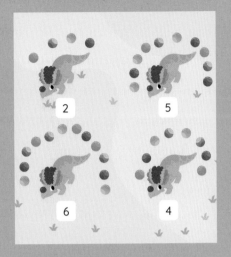

2
5
6
4

## 40 Two by two

12 − 10 = 2    5 − 2 = 3
2 + 2 = 4    11 − 8 = 3
8 − 5 = 3    2 − 0 = 2
2 + 0 = 2    6 − 6 = 0
7 − 3 = 4    2 − 1 = 1
9 − 6 = 3    7 − 6 = 1

## 41 Big night out

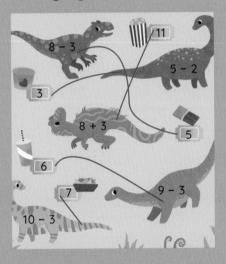

11
8 − 3
5 − 2
3
8 + 3
5
6
7
9 − 3
10 − 3

## 42 Equal to the task

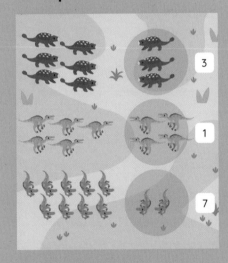

3
1
7

## 43 Grubbing around

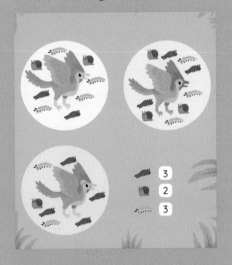

3
2
3

## 44 Head count

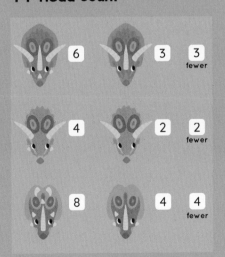

6    3    3 fewer
4    2    2 fewer
8    4    4 fewer

## 45 Fishing frenzy

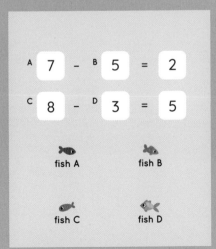

A 7 − B 5 = 2
C 8 − D 3 = 5

fish A     fish B

fish C     fish D

## 46 All change

How many chrysalis are hanging in picture 1?  12

How many chrysalis are hanging in picture 2?  8

How many blue butterflies are there in picture 1?  10

How many blue butterflies are there in picture 2?  7

What is the difference between the two numbers?  4

What is the total number of blue butterflies in both pictures?  17

## 47 More or less?

| A | B | Difference | |
|---|---|---|---|
| 8 | 4 | 4 | (more) / less |
| 11 | 12 | 1 | more / (less) |
| 8 | 5 | 3 | (more) / less |
| 6 | 4 | 2 | (more) / less |
| 13 | 6 | 7 | (more) / less |
| 3 | 8 | 5 | more / (less) |
| 4 | 2 | 2 | (more) / less |
| 8 | 14 | 6 | more / (less) |

## 48 On the move

10
20  30
40
50
60
70  80

This is the total distance Dina walks.
80

## 49 In a flap

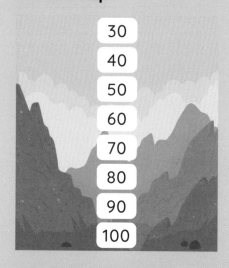

30
40
50
60
70
80
90
100

## 50 All the tens

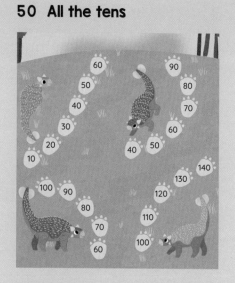

60
50
40
30
20
10
90
80
70
100
90
80
70
60
140
130
120
110
100
40  50

## 51 Art school

30

55

48

## 52 Gone fishing

| 6 | + | 10 | = | 16 |
| 2 | + | 10 | = | 12 |
| 8 | + | 10 | = | 18 |
| 9 | + | 10 | = | 19 |
| 5 | + | 10 | = | 15 |
| 4 | + | 10 | = | 14 |

## 53 Fetch!

| 15 | 25 | 35 | 45 | 55 |
| 18 | 28 | 38 | 48 | 58 |
| 26 | 36 | 46 | 56 | 66 |

## 54 Strange creatures

## 55 Fossil finds

2  4  6  8
10
12
24  22  20  18  16  14
26
28
30
32
34  36  38  40

## 56 Bigger bonds

| 18 | + | 2 | = | 20 |
|----|---|---|---|----|
| 17 | + | 3 | = | 20 |
| 6 | + | 14 | = | 20 |
| 5 | + | 15 | = | 20 |
| 16 | + | 4 | = | 20 |

## 57 Perfect partners

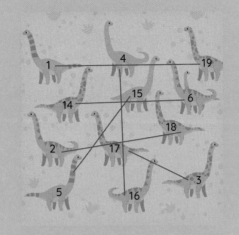

1   4   19
15   6
14
18
2   17
3
5   16

## 58 Back to class

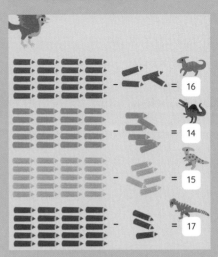

- = 16
- = 14
- = 15
- = 17

## 59 Feeling fruitful

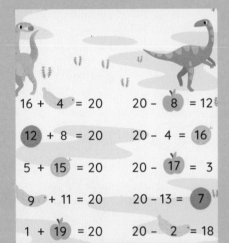

16 + 4 = 20     20 − 8 = 12

12 + 8 = 20     20 − 4 = 16

5 + 15 = 20     20 − 17 = 3

9 + 11 = 20     20 − 13 = 7

1 + 19 = 20     20 − 2 = 18

## 60 Add them up

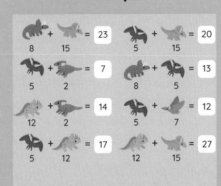

| + | = 23 | | + | = 20 |
| 8 | 15 | | 5 | 15 |
| + | = 7 | | + | = 13 |
| 5 | 2 | | 8 | 5 |
| + | = 14 | | + | = 12 |
| 12 | 2 | | 5 | 7 |
| + | = 17 | | + | = 27 |
| 5 | 12 | | 12 | 15 |

## 61 Super speedy

11 + 6 = 17     13 + 1 = 14

14 + 5 = 19     16 + 4 = 20

12 + 3 = 15     10 + 9 = 19

11 + 4 = 15     12 + 5 = 17

22 + 1 = 23     17 + 2 = 19

25 + 0 = 25     11 + 8 = 19

## 62 Bridging through 10

6 + 7 = 13

10
+4      +3
6      7      13

8 + 5 = 13

10
+2      +3
8      5      13

9 + 6 = 15

10
+1      +5
9      6      15

## 63 Bridging back

16 − 7 = 9

10
−6      −1
16      7      9

13 − 6 = 7

10
−3      −3
13      6      7

15 − 8 = 7

10
−5      −3
15      8      7

## 64 Happy families

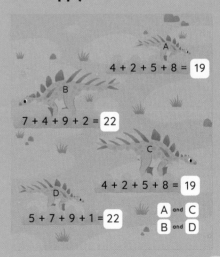

A
4 + 2 + 5 + 8 = 19

B
7 + 4 + 9 + 2 = 22

C
4 + 2 + 5 + 8 = 19

D
5 + 7 + 9 + 1 = 22

A and C
B and D

## 65  T. rex teaser

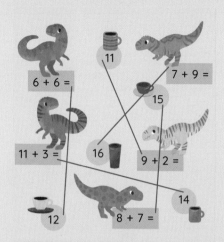

6 + 6 =
11
7 + 9 =
15
11 + 3 =
16
9 + 2 =
14
12
8 + 7 =

## 66  Safety in numbers

100 − 20 = **80**

100 − 50 = **50**

100 − 70 = **30**

100 − 90 = **10**

100 − 100 = **0**

## 67  Plodding along

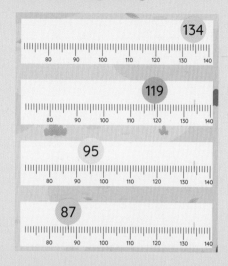

## 68  Star students

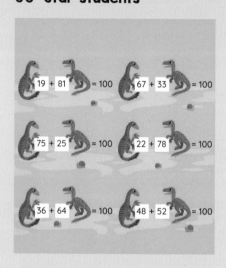

19 + 81 = 100    67 + 33 = 100

75 + 25 = 100    22 + 78 = 100

36 + 64 = 100    48 + 52 = 100

## 69  Winging it

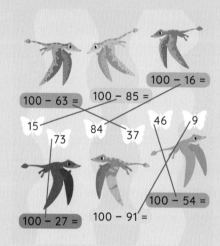

100 − 16 =
100 − 85 =
100 − 63 =
15    84    37
73    46    9
100 − 54 =
100 − 27 =    100 − 91 =

## 70  Doubling up

20
40  44
22
33    66  99  133
400    80  880  800

## 71  Half and half

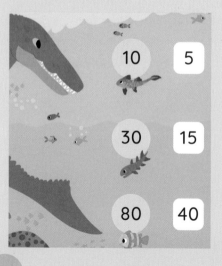

10    5

30    15

80    40

## 72  Three by three

| 23 | + | 29 | = | 52 |
|----|---|----|---|----|
| 29 | + | 23 | = | 52 |
| 52 | − | 23 | = | 29 |
| 52 | − | 29 | = | 23 |

| 16 | + | 25 | = | 41 |
|----|---|----|---|----|
| 25 | + | 16 | = | 41 |
| 41 | − | 16 | = | 15 |
| 41 | − | 25 | = | 16 |

| 13 | + | 15 | = | 28 |
|----|---|----|---|----|
| 15 | + | 13 | = | 28 |
| 28 | − | 13 | = | 15 |
| 28 | − | 15 | = | 13 |

| 19 | + | 44 | = | 63 |
|----|---|----|---|----|
| 44 | + | 19 | = | 63 |
| 63 | − | 19 | = | 44 |
| 63 | − | 44 | = | 19 |

## 73 Triceratops tricks

| 21 | + | 18 | = | 39 |
|----|---|----|---|----|
| 18 | + | 21 | = | 39 |
| 39 | – | 18 | = | 21 |
| 39 | – | 21 | = | (14) |

| 11 | + | 25 | = | 36 |
|----|---|----|---|----|
| 25 | + | 11 | = | 36 |
| 36 | – | 11 | = | (22) |
| 36 | – | 25 | = | 11 |

| 24 | + | 32 | = | 56 |
|----|---|----|---|----|
| 32 | + | 24 | = | 56 |
| (54) | – | 24 | = | 32 |
| 56 | – | 32 | = | 24 |

| 28 | + | 49 | = | 77 |
|----|---|----|---|----|
| (47) | + | 28 | = | 77 |
| 77 | – | 49 | = | 28 |
| 77 | – | 28 | = | 49 |

## 74 Higher and lower

| ten more (add 10) | | ten less (subtract 10) |
|----|----|----|
| 25 | 15 | 5 |
| 52 | 42 | 32 |
| 87 | 77 | 67 |
| 31 | 21 | 11 |
| 49 | 39 | 29 |
| 66 | 56 | 46 |
| 75 | 65 | 55 |
| 100 | 90 | 80 |
| 122 | 112 | 102 |

## 75 Top of the class

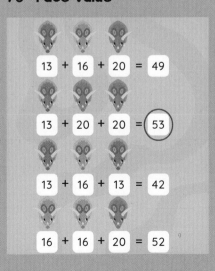

Double 8

6 + 10

90—74

12 + 4

50—34

Half of 32

(11 + 15)

88—72

94

69—53

## 76 Tread carefully

34
14
44
24
54
94
84
74
64

## 77 Fishy fun

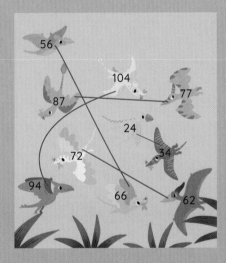

56
104
87
77
24
34
72
94
66
62

## 78 Face value

| 13 | + | 16 | + | 20 | = | 49 |
|----|---|----|---|----|---|----|
| 13 | + | 20 | + | 20 | = | (53) |
| 13 | + | 16 | + | 13 | = | 42 |
| 16 | + | 16 | + | 20 | = | 52 |

## 79 Prehistoric puzzler

60
22
15
40
38
25

## 80 Carnotaurus columns

| | Hundreds | Tens | Units |
|-----|----------|------|-------|
| 3 | 0 | 0 | 3 |
| 33 | 0 | 3 | 3 |
| 300 | 3 | 0 | 0 |
| 13 | 0 | 1 | 3 |
| 15 | 0 | 1 | 5 |
| 155 | 1 | 5 | 5 |
| 500 | 5 | 0 | 0 |
| 505 | 5 | 0 | 5 |
| 555 | 5 | 5 | 5 |

## 81 Write it right

12 − 3 = 9

30 − 16 = 14

18 + 18 = 36

2 + 2 + 2 + 2 + 2 + 2 + 2 + 2 + 2 + 2 = 20

## 82 Use your brain

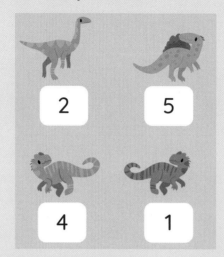

2

5

4

1

## 83 Dinosaur friends

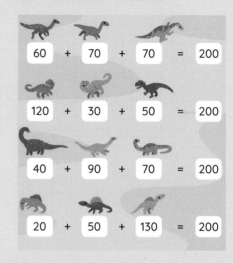

60 + 70 + 70 = 200

120 + 30 + 50 = 200

40 + 90 + 70 = 200

20 + 50 + 130 = 200

## 84 How much?

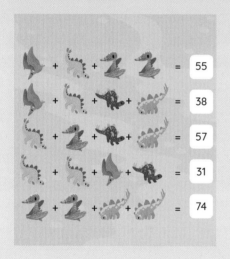

+ + + = 55

+ + + = 38

+ + + = 57

+ + + = 31

+ + + = 74

## 85 Take it away

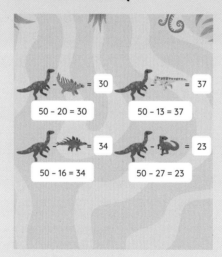

− = 30    50 − 20 = 30

− = 37    50 − 13 = 37

− = 34    50 − 16 = 34

− = 23    50 − 27 = 23

## 86 End of the line

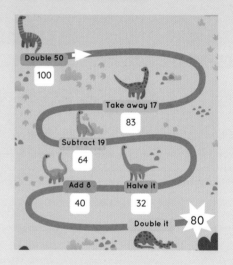

Double 50

100

Take away 17

83

Subtract 19

64

Add 8

40

Halve it

32

Double it    80

96